# Odd Ball

## Hilarious, Unusual, & Bizarre Baseball Moments

by **Timothy Tocher** illustrated by **Stacy Curtis**

*Marshall Cavendish Children*

## Acknowledgments

Stacy would like to thank his wife, Jann, for her help in scanning images for this book.

Special thanks also to Andrew Gmitter, for his review and comments on the text and artwork.

The following reference was helpful in researching the players' uniforms: *Baseball Uniforms of the 20th Century: The Official Major League Baseball Guide* by Marc Okkonen (Sterling, 1993).

Marshall Cavendish Corporation, 99 White Plains Road, Tarrytown, NY 10591
www.marshallcavendish.us/kids

Library of Congress Cataloging-in-Publication Data
Tocher, Timothy.
Odd ball : hilarious, unusual, and bizarre baseball moments / by Timothy Tocher ;
illustrated by Stacy Curtis.
p. cm.
ISBN 978-0-7614-5813-5
1. Baseball—United States—Miscellanea—Juvenile literature. I. Curtis, Stacy ill. II. Title.
GV867.5.T63 2011
796.357—dc22
2010013847

The illustrations are rendered in pen and ink.
Book design by Virginia Pope
Editor: Marilyn Brigham

Printed in China (E)
First edition
10 9 8 7 6 5 4 3 2 1

For Colin, Ella, and Emma—
three great additions to any team
                                    —T. T.

For the baseball fans on 50$^{th}$ Court
                                    —S. C.

# Contents

# ALL EARS

**W**hen rating a ballplayer, scouts look for a strong throwing arm, powerful legs, and keen eyesight. No one checks a player's ears. Yet ears, too, can play a role in the game.

# ENTERTAINING EARS

In 1964 the New York Mets had a new ballpark but the same losing team. How could they draw fans to Shea Stadium?

RIGHT FIELDER JOE CHRISTOPHER DID HIS PART.

THE 29-YEAR-OLD BATTED .300 WHILE BANGING OUT 50 EXTRA-BASE HITS.
POW!

STILL, MANY GAMES GOT OUT OF HAND.

TO KEEP HIMSELF AMUSED, JOE WOULD PRACTICE WIGGLING HIS EARS.

FANS NOTICED AND SOON BEGAN CALLING FOR JOE'S SPECIALTY.
HAT TRICK! HAT TRICK! HAT TRICK! HAT TRICK!

MANAGER CASEY STENGEL LOVED IT.
THAT'S USING YOUR HEAD!

# A REAL EARACHE

"Sweet Lou" Johnson, a Dodger hero of the mid-sixties, had three ears. Or so he claimed. Lou played in the minor leagues for 10 long seasons and acquired his third ear during a bus ride across Mexico.

# MELTON MELTDOWN

Cliff Melton was a rangy lefthander with great stuff, yet he won only 6 more games than he lost while pitching for the Giants from 1937-1944. Could his ears have been to blame?

In those days, most fans were men, and most men wore white shirts to the ballpark. It was hard for a batter to spot the baseball as it left the pitcher's hand with all of those white shirts behind him. Hitters claimed that Cliff's huge, floppy ears blocked out the white shirts and gave hitters a perfect view of the baseball.

William E. Hoy's ears led to the creation of the hand signals that indicate strike or ball, out or safe, fair or foul. A star of the late 1800s, Hoy could neither hear nor speak. Hall of Fame umpire Bill Klem invented the gestures to help Hoy track the events of the game.

# 2nd Inning

# THIS GAME IS FOR THE BIRDS

**M**ajor League Baseball wouldn't be the same without the Orioles, Cardinals, and Blue Jays. Yet, when other types of birds visit the ballpark, all sorts of wacky events occur.

# FEATHERED FANS

No one knows why hundreds of seagulls made Jacobs Field in Cleveland their hango[r]
early in the 2009 season. Maybe they were fans of the Indians.

# FAST FOOD?

At Comiskey Park in 1945, one White Sox fan found a unique way to motivate a player.

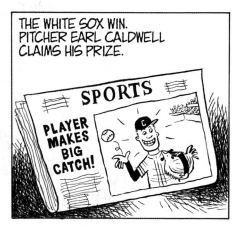

# WINGED SALUTE

Brooklyn fans were heartbroken when Casey Stengel was traded to the Pittsburgh Pirates. On May 25, 1919, a large crowd packed Ebbets Field to see Casey return as an opposing player.

CASEY TROTS TO HIS POSITION IN RIGHT FIELD.

HE FINDS AN INJURED SPARROW ON THE GRASS.

CASEY PUTS THE BIRD IN A SAFE PLACE.

WHEN CASEY COMES TO BAT, THE CROWD GIVES HIM A WARM GREETING.

CASEY TIPS HIS CAP.

THE FANS ERUPT INTO A STANDING OVATION.

James "Jim" Murray, head of the Philadelphia Zoo in 1883, came up with a unique way to get up-to-the-minute reports on his beloved Phillies during their inaugural season. Jim sent a zoo employee to home games carrying a cage filled with carrier pigeons. At the end of each inning, the employee would write a brief update and attach it to the leg of one of the birds. Once released, the pigeon would fly straight to its home at the zoo, and Jim would read the message.

# THE ULTIMATE HIGH POP

**H**ave you ever staggered around the infield, waiting for a pop fly to come down? Imagine trying to catch one of these.

# MONUMENTAL ACHIEVEMENT

In 1888, the newly constructed Washington Monument was the tallest building in the world. Baseballers debated whether a ball dropped from its 504-foot-high observation deck could be caught.

The Washington Monument gets wider from top to bottom. Balls dropped from the top would bounce off the walls before reaching the base. These balls were hard to locate and judge. Schriver's feat was duplicated in 1908 and again in 1910, but each time it took far more than two attempts.

# THE PLANE TRUTH

If you brag about your exploits on the diamond, you may be asked to prove yourself.

BROOKLYN MANAGER AND FORMER CATCHER WILBERT ROBINSON LOSES HIS TEMPER WHEN A PLAYER MISSES A POP FLY.

BUT IT WAS WAY UP THERE.

SO? I COULD CATCH A BALL DROPPED FROM AN AIRPLANE.

WHEN FEMALE STUNT PILOT RUTH LAW IS HIRED TO PERFORM AT SPRING TRAINING, THE PLAYERS CHALLENGE ROBINSON TO BACK UP HIS BOAST.

ROBINSON GAMELY TAKES HIS POSITION.

AS RUTH CIRCLES THE FIELD, SHE REALIZES SHE FORGOT A BASEBALL.

THIS GRAPEFRUIT I WAS GOING TO EAT FOR LUNCH WILL HAVE TO DO.

ROBINSON MAKES THE CATCH.

SPLAT!

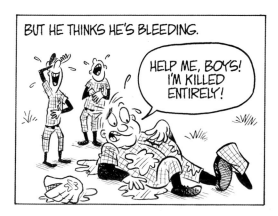

BUT HE THINKS HE'S BLEEDING.

HELP ME, BOYS! I'M KILLED ENTIRELY!

# GABBY AND THE BLIMP

The Goodyear Tire and Rubber Company launched its first blimp in 1925. It was only a matter of time until someone tried to catch a baseball dropped from it.

AS A BOY, GABBY HARTNETT NEARLY LOST HIS CHANCE TO PLAY IN THE MAJOR LEAGUES BECAUSE OF AN ACCIDENT.

GABBY'S ARM DIDN'T HEAL PROPERLY. HIS PARENTS HAD 13 OTHER CHILDREN, AND NO MONEY TO PAY A DOCTOR.

GABBY'S MOTHER HAD AN IDEA THAT COULD STRENGTHEN HIS ARM.

CARRY THIS PAIL OF SAND WHEREVER YOU GO.

THE HOME REMEDY WORKED. GABBY BECAME A STAR CATCHER WITH THE CHICAGO CUBS.

APRIL 1, 1930: GABBY ATTEMPTS TO CATCH A BASEBALL DROPPED 800 FEET FROM THE BLIMP.

GABBY CATCHES THE FIRST BALL, AND MINUTES LATER, CATCHES A SECOND.

In 1939, at the San Francisco Golden Gate Exposition, veteran minor league catcher Joe Sprinz tried to duplicate Gabby Hartnett's feat. Joe made the mistake of holding his mitt in front of his face. The speeding baseball drove the mitt into his jaw, knocking out two teeth and breaking his cheekbone. It's no surprise that he dropped the ball.

# ODDBALL PITCHERS

**T**he pitchers in this chapter must have been extremely talented. Why else would their teammates put up with them?

# WILDMAN WADDELL

George Edward "Rube" Waddell led the American League in strikeouts every year from 1902-1907, yet he still infuriated his managers.

SOME DAYS RUBE NEVER MADE IT TO THE BALLPARK.

RUBE WOULD MISS A GAME TO SEE A FIRE.

ON ROAD TRIPS, PLAYERS SLEPT TWO TO A BED TO SAVE MONEY. NO ONE WANTED TO ROOM WITH RUBE.

CRUNCH! CRUNCH!

AS A JOKE, RUBE WOULD SCOOP UP HIS OWN FOOT INSTEAD OF THE BALL.

BUT THEN RUBE WOULD USUALLY STRIKE OUT THE NEXT BATTER.

NO HARM DONE.

WHEN RUBE WORE OUT HIS WELCOME IN THE BIG LEAGUES, HE TOOK UP A NEW PROFESSION.

# "JAWS" BORBON

Pedro pitched in relief for the Cincinnati Reds from 1970-1979, twice helping them win the World Series. Despite his success, Pedro occasionally bit off more than he could chew.

1973: THE METS AND REDS ARE IN A PLAYOFF TO SEE WHICH TEAM WILL GO TO THE WORLD SERIES. THE METS ARE WINNING WHEN PETE ROSE SLAMS INTO NEW YORK'S BUD HARRELSON AT SECOND.

A FIGHT BREAKS OUT.

PEDRO RUNS IN FROM THE BULLPEN TO JOIN THE FRAY.

PEDRO SQUARES OFF WITH METS PITCHER BUZZ CAPRA.

AT LAST, ORDER IS RESTORED. IN THE CONFUSION, PEDRO PUTS ON A METS CAP.

PEDRO PULLS OFF THE CAP TO SEE WHY IT DOESN'T FIT.

Pedro's strong bite earned him the nicknames the "Dominican Dracula" and "Jaws."

# A BIRD FLIES HIGH IN DETROIT

In spring training of 1976, Detroit Tigers rookie Mark Fidrych was considered more of an oddity than a pitcher.... Then the season started.

Only 23 years old, Mark pitched in the All-Star game, was named American League Rookie of the Year, and won 19 games while losing only 6. The following March, Mark twisted his knee in spring training. Arm injuries followed. Fidrych pitched until 1983, but won only 10 more games.

In 1911, a Kansas farmer named Victory Faust consulted a fortune-teller. She predicted he would pitch the New York Giants to the National League pennant. Even though he wasn't a baseball player, Faust hopped a train to St. Louis where the Giants were playing. Manager John McGraw found Faust amusing and kept him with the team as a good luck charm. The Giants won the pennant three years in a row. The following season, Faust left the team. The Giants finished in sixth place.

5th Inning

# UNEXPECTED EVENTS

**T**eam owners constantly search for new ways to attract fans. Their creative ideas have led to many baseball oddities.

# INCH HITTER

Why would oddball owner Bill Veeck's 1951 St. Louis Browns use a pinch hitter in the very first inning of a game?

The Browns used a pinch runner for Gaedel. The next day, the rules were changed so that no player could be signed without the approval of the league president. Eddie Gaedel's career was over.

# YOU NEVER SAUSAGE A RACE

Since 1994, fans of the Milwaukee Brewers have been treated to a "Sausage Race" along with the ballgame. On July 9, 2003, Pittsburgh Pirates' first baseman Randall Simon took too strong an interest in which sausage won.

A woman named Mandy Block was wearing the Italian Sausage costume. She asked Randall Simon for the bat he had used to bop her. He handed it over with an autograph and an apology.

# BARACKLYN, NEW YORK

Steve Cohen, General Manager of the Brooklyn Cyclones, a farm team of the New York Mets, declared June 23, 2009 Baracklyn Night. Steve planned to honor President Obama, the USA's first African-American president, and to draw a crowd to Keyspan Park.

A LINE OF FANS STRETCHES TWO BLOCKS DOWN SURF AVENUE.

THE FIRST 2,500 FANS ARE GIVEN A SOUVENIR.

FANS NAMED BARACK ARE ADMITTED FREE. ONLY ONE SHOWS UP.

RANDALL WEST, A PRESIDENT OBAMA LOOK-ALIKE, THROWS THE FIRST PITCH.

THE CYCLONES WEAR SPECIAL UNIFORMS. ONE WILL BE DISPLAYED AT THE BASEBALL HALL OF FAME IN COOPERSTOWN, NEW YORK.

BARACKLYN DEFEATS THE HUDSON VALLEY RENEGADES 7-3.

As part of the opening day celebration at Yankee Stadium in 1978, every fan was given a Reggie Bar, a new confection named in honor of slugger Reggie Jackson. If fans had gobbled them up, there would have been no problem. But most people decided to keep the colorful sweet as a souvenir. Then Reggie hit a home run. In their excitement, the fans threw thousands of candy bars onto the field. The game had to be stopped while the grounds crew cleaned up the mess.

# 6th Inning

# FOUR-LEGGED FANS

**D**oesn't it get your goat when people bring their doggone animals to the ballpark? Enjoy these odd moments involving pets and mascots.

# A HOWLING SUCCESS

Slugger Dan Brouthers starred for several teams in the 1890s. Wherever Dan traveled, an Irish setter named Kelly kept him company.

FOR MOST OF THE GAME, KELLY TAKES IT EASY.

WHEN HER OWNER COMES TO BAT, SHE TAKES MORE INTEREST.

THE ORIOLES ARE DOWN TO THEIR LAST OUT. DAN CRUSHES A FASTBALL.

TAKE THAT!

THE TYING RUN SCORES AS DAN ROUNDS THIRD.

OHWOOO!

DAN SLIDES HOME WITH THE WINNING RUN.

KELLY CELEBRATES IN HER OWN STYLE.

# THE GOAT CURSE

William Sianis was a rabid fan of the Chicago Cubs. When the team faced the Detroit Tigers in the 1945 World Series, Sianis bought a pair of box seats for game 4. The Cubs needed just 2 more wins to clinch the championship. The problem came when Sianis invited his best friend, Murphy, to the game.

SIANIS AND MURPHY WALK TO WRIGLEY FIELD.

THE FRIENDS ARE TURNED AWAY AT THE TURNSTILE.

GET THAT SMELLY CREATURE OUT OF HERE!

BUT HE'S GOT A TICKET.

NO GOATS ALLOWED.

THEN I CURSE THIS TEAM. MAY THE CUBS NEVER AGAIN WIN THE WORLD SERIES.

MURPHY SNEAKS IN A SNACK BEFORE LEAVING.

THE TIGERS WIN 3 OF THE NEXT 4 GAMES TO TAKE THE TITLE.

HA! HA!

TO REVERSE THE CURSE, IN 1984 WILLIAM'S NEPHEW SAM SIANIS WAS INVITED TO BRING A GOAT TO WRIGLEY FIELD. BUT THE CUBS HAVE YET TO MAKE IT BACK TO THE WORLD SERIES.

# MIXED-UP MASCOT

In their second season, 1963, the Mets thought that a mascot might bring them luck. They chose a handsome beagle and named him Homer. The plan was for Homer to circle the bases every time a Met hit a home run.

Poor Homer was fired shortly after the game.

There were no dogs allowed in American League Park in Washington, DC, in 1900, but there was a doghouse in center field. It was used to store the American flag. Outfielder Ralph "Socks" Seybold of the Philadelphia As was chasing a long drive when the baseball bounced into the doghouse. His arm was too short to reach the ball, so Socks forced his head and shoulders through the small opening. When he was unable to get out, the batter scored an inside-the-park home run.

# 7th Inning

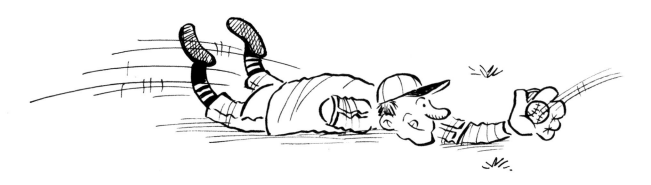

# MISSING AND SPARE PARTS

**W**e think of professional athletes as perfect specimens, yet a few individuals have mastered the skills necessary to become major leaguers despite physical abnormalities.

# WITHOUT A LEG TO STAND ON

Fans in Boston were watching the Washington Senators take batting practice on a lazy summer afternoon in 1945 when something unexpected happened.

PITCHER BERT SHEPARD'S RIGHT FOOT FALLS OFF.

THE SPECTATORS GASP, BUT BERT'S TEAMMATES LAUGH. THEY KNOW BERT HAS AN ARTIFICIAL LEG.

HA! HA!

BERT HAD LEFT BASEBALL TO SERVE AS A FIGHTER PILOT IN WORLD WAR II. ON A MISSION, HIS PLANE WAS SHOT DOWN. DOCTORS REMOVED BERT'S RIGHT LEG TO SAVE HIS LIFE.

FITTED WITH AN ARTIFICIAL LEG, BERT RESUMED PITCHING. THE SENATORS HIRED HIM TO COACH AND PITCH BATTING PRACTICE.

AUGUST 4, 1945: THE SENATORS TRAILED THE RED SOX BY 12 RUNS. BERT WAS BROUGHT IN TO PITCH WITH THE BASES LOADED AND TWO OUTS.

STRIKE THREE!

Bert pitched 4 more innings that day, allowing only 1 run. After the season he quit his coaching job and returned to the minor leagues, where he pitched and played first base for 9 seasons.

# THE ONE-ARMED OUTFIELDER

May 20, 1945: At Sportsman's Park, St. Louis, Browns rookie Pete Gray had a spectacular day against the New York Yankees.

IN A DOUBLEHEADER, PETE GETS 4 BASE HITS AND MAKES 3 SENSATIONAL CATCHES, DESPITE HAVING ONLY ONE ARM.

WHEN HE WAS 6 YEARS OLD, PETE LOST AN ARM IN A TRUCK ACCIDENT. HE TAUGHT HIMSELF TO PLAY BASEBALL ONE-HANDED.

BATTING .333 AND LEADING THE MINOR LEAGUES IN STOLEN BASES IN THE 1944 SEASON EARNED PETE A PROMOTION TO THE BIG LEAGUES.

PETE HAS A GREAT SENSE OF HUMOR.

HAVE I WORKED ON YOU BEFORE?

NO. I GOT THIS IN A MOTOR ACCIDENT.

HAIR CUTS

Sadly, Pete's early success didn't last. Taking advantage of the fact that Pete had little hitting power, opposing defenses played more and more shallow. Balls that had dropped in for hits early in the season were now caught. By the end of the year, Pete's batting average was down to .218 and his days as a major leaguer were over.

# JIM ABBOTT

Although courageous and talented, Bert Shepard and Pete Gray saw their only big league action in 1945, when hundreds of players were serving in the military. Jim Abbott pitched in the major leagues for 11 seasons, despite being born with one hand.

JIM WENT STRAIGHT FROM THE UNIVERSITY OF MICHIGAN TO THE CALIFORNIA ANGELS WITHOUT EVER PITCHING IN THE MINOR LEAGUES.

JIM PITCHED WITH HIS MITT BALANCED ON HIS RIGHT WRIST. AS SOON AS HE LET GO OF THE BASEBALL, HE SLID HIS LEFT HAND INTO THE MITT AND WAS READY TO FIELD HIS POSITION.

HE WON 12 GAMES AS A ROOKIE AND AS MANY AS 18 IN ONE SEASON.

PITCHING FOR THE YANKEES IN 1993, JIM THREW A NO-HITTER.

SINCE THE AMERICAN LEAGUE USES A DESIGNATED HITTER, JIM SELDOM CAME TO BAT.

BUT HE ONCE HIT A 400-FOOT DOUBLE IN AN EXHIBITION GAME.

Relief pitcher Antonio Alfonseca was given more than his share. Born with 6 fingers on each hand and 6 toes on each foot, Antonio led the league in digits every season of his 13-year career. His teammates on the 1997 World Champion Florida Marlins nicknamed him "Pulpo," the Spanish word for octopus.

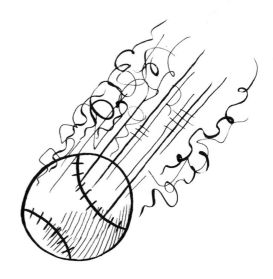

# 8th Inning

# FREAKY FOULS

Stay alert in the stands. At any moment a baseball may come flying at you. The result could be a souvenir, a nasty bump, or something even stranger. . . .

# DOESN'T THAT BURN YOU UP?

Players try to "light a fire" in their fans. In August, 1915, the aptly named George Burns of the Cleveland Indians carried things a little too far.

BURNS FOULS A BALL INTO THE SEATS.

THE BALL HITS A POCKET FULL OF MATCHES.

I'M BURNING!

YIKES!

A VENDOR COMES TO THE RESCUE.

SHAKE! SHAKE! SHAKE!

I ALWAYS WANTED TO BE A FIREMAN.

# ASHBURN'S DOUBLE WHAMMY

On August 17, 1957, Alice Roth visited Shibe Park in Philadelphia to cheer for her beloved Phillies. Alice had a great seat, right behind third base.

# FINDERS KEEPERS

In baseball's early days, fans were expected to return a baseball that was hit into the stands. An incident at Yankee Stadium in 1934 changed that custom.

MIGHTY LOU GEHRIG FOULS A BALL INTO THE SECOND DECK. DAVID LEVY MAKES THE CATCH.

GOT IT!

WHAT A PRIZE!

THE CHASE IS ON.

LEVY IS CORNERED.

IT'S MINE!

HE REACHES THE TIPPING POINT.

LEVY SUES THE YANKEES AND MAJOR LEAGUE BASEBALL, SETTLING FOR $7,500.

Since David Levy's lawsuit, fans have been allowed to keep caught balls as souvenirs. On May 31, 1964, the New York Mets must have been tempted to reconsider this policy. The team hosted an odd doubleheader against the San Francisco Giants. The second game went 23 innings before the Giants managed an 8-6 victory. A record 264 baseballs were used.

# GET YOUR MITTS OFF ME!

**U**ntil 1870, players fielded barehanded. Then Doug Allison of the Cincinnati Red Stockings started a game wearing "buckskin mittens to protect his hands," as reported in the *Cincinnati Commercial* newspaper. As you may have guessed, Doug was a catcher. Mitts prevented injuries, so their use gradually spread to other positions. But that doesn't mean they didn't create their own set of odd occurrences.

# HOOPER'S HOT POTATO

Hall-of-Famer Harry Hooper led the Boston Red Sox to 4 World Series appearances between 1912 and 1918.

HARRY HOOPER WAS A GOOD HITTER, BUT IT WAS HIS FIELDING THAT MADE HIM A STAR.

HARRY WAS A STUDENT OF THE GAME. HE READ THAT BASE RUNNERS WERE NOT ALLOWED TO ADVANCE ON A FLY OUT UNTIL THE FIELDER HAD "CAUGHT THE BASEBALL." THAT GAVE HIM AN IDEA.

WITH A RUNNER LEADING OFF THIRD, THE BATTER HITS A FLY BALL TO HOOPER.

INSTEAD OF CATCHING THE BALL, HARRY SLAPS IT INTO THE AIR AND TOWARD THE INFIELD.

SLAP!

THE BASE RUNNER IS FROZEN.

HARRY SLAPS THE BALL INTO THE AIR A SECOND AND THIRD TIME. ONLY WHEN HE REACHES THE INFIELD DOES HE MAKE THE CATCH.

WANT TO TRY TO RUN?

Major League Baseball had to rewrite the rule. Now, batters are permitted to "tag up" as soon as the baseball touches a fielder.

# THE GREAT LOMBARDI

A catcher's mitt has more padding than the glove of any other player, unless the catcher is Hall-of-Famer Ernie Lombardi. He played for the Reds, Dodgers, Braves, and Giants in a career spanning the years 1931-1947.

ERNIE WAS THE SLOWEST RUNNER EVER TO PLAY IN THE MAJOR LEAGUES. BEHIND THE PLATE, HE COULDN'T SHIFT QUICKLY ENOUGH TO BLOCK PITCHES.

SO ERNIE REMOVED ALL THE PADDING FROM HIS MITT. BALLS TO HIS LEFT, HE SCOOPED LIKE A FIRST BASEMAN.

PITCHES TO HIS RIGHT, HE CAUGHT IN HIS BARE HAND.

ERNIE'S RIGHT HAND BARELY LOOKED HUMAN.

ERNIE'S BULK HELPED WHEN HE BLOCKED THE PLATE.

A skilled and powerful hitter, Ernie is the only catcher to win 2 batting championships. In 1938, he was named the Most Valuable Player in the National League. Lombardi's nickname was "The Schnozz." Ernie's nose was so long that the tip stuck through the bars of his catcher's mask, and was often scratched and bruised.

# FEARFUL PHIL

Once gloves became standard equipment, players had to decide what to do with them when their team was at bat. For years, they left them on the ground near their position. A quirky shortstop named Phil Rizzuto changed all that.

PHIL GREW UP IN NEW YORK CITY. HE ASKED FOR TRYOUTS WITH THE GIANTS AND DODGERS.

GO HOME, KID. YOU'RE TOO SMALL.

NO BOYS ALLOWED.

BUT THE YANKEES GAVE PHIL A CHANCE.

SLICK FIELDING AND SKILLED HITTING MADE PHIL A STAR.

AN OPPONENT NOTICED THAT PHIL WAS AFRAID OF CRAWLY THINGS.

OPPOSING PLAYERS PUT ANTS, EARTHWORMS, AND OTHER CRITTERS IN PHIL'S GLOVE TO THROW HIM OFF HIS GAME.

PHIL WANTED TO BRING HIS GLOVE INTO THE DUGOUT BETWEEN INNINGS, BUT HE KNEW IT WOULD INVITE MORE RIDICULE. SO HE ASKED HIS TEAMMATES TO JOIN HIM.

The Yankees were so successful, winning 5 consecutive World Series from 1947-1951, that other teams copied everything they did. Before long, no one left his glove on the field. Able to concentrate on baseball, Phil won the American League Most Valuable Player Award in 1950.

Bid McPhee played second base for the Reds from 1882–1899. He played barehanded until 1896, when a broken finger forced him to wear a glove to protect his injury. The final holdout was Gus Weyhing, who pitched until 1901 and never wore a mitt.

# ODD FACTS ABOUT THE PLAYERS

**ABBOTT, JIM** (1967-    )

Each spring Jim helps prepare the California Angels pitching staff for the coming season. The rest of the year, he travels the country as a motivational speaker.

**ALFONSECA, ANTONIO** (1972-    )

Antonio's grandfather was also polydactyl. That is, he had 6 fingers on each hand and 6 toes on each foot.

**ASHBURN, RICHARD** (1927-1997)

After his playing career, Richie became a radio and television announcer for the Phillies.

**BORBON, PEDRO "JAWS"** (1967-    )

It wasn't only Pedro's teeth that were exceptionally strong. During pregame warm-ups, Pedro loved to stand on the warning track in center field and pitch strikes to the catcher at home plate.

**BROUTHERS, DENNIS "DAN"** (1858-1932)

Kelly must have done many backflips, since Dan won 5 batting championships.

**BURNS, GEORGE** (1893-1978)

George played for 16 seasons and set fire to only one fan.

**CHOO, SHIN-SOO** (1982-    )

Playing for his native South Korea, Choo was named MVP of the 2000 Junior World Baseball Championships.

## CHRISTOPHER, JOSEPH (1935-    )

Joe was the first player from the Virgin Islands to play in the major leagues.

## CRAMER, ROGER "DOC" (1905-1990)

Doc Cramer Boulevard, a street in Manahawkin, NJ, was named in Doc's honor.

## FAUST, CHARLES VICTOR "VICTORY" (1880-1915)

Faust appeared on the vaudeville stage, demonstrating his pitching technique and telling stories about his experiences with the Giants.

## FIDRYCH, MARK "THE BIRD" (1954-2009)

Mark's fans called themselves "The Bird Watchers."

## GRAY, PETER (1915-2002)

Pete struck out only 11 times in 234 at-bats in the major leagues.

## HARTNETT, CHARLES "GABBY" (1900-1972)

Hartnett was painfully shy. His teammates called him "Gabby" because he seldom spoke.

## HOOPER, HARRY (1887-1974)

"Hoop, Hoop, Hooper Up for Red Sox" was a popular song in 1915.

## HOY, WILLIAM (1862-1961)

In 2001 Gallaudet University, a school for the hearing impaired, named their baseball diamond "Hoy Field."

## JACKSON, REGINALD (1946-   )

In game 6 of the 1977 World Series, Reggie hit 3 home runs in 3 at-bats. Each came on the first pitch thrown to him.

## JOHNSON, LOUIS (1934-   )

Lou celebrated home runs by clapping his hands as he circled the bases. Opposing pitchers did not like it. Lou was hit by a pitch as many as 16 times in one season.

## LOMBARDI, ERNIE (1908-1977)

In 1938, Johnny Vandermeer of the Reds pitched no-hitters in 2 consecutive starts, a feat that has never been equaled. Ernie caught both games.

## MELTON, CLIFF (1912-1986)

"Mickey Mouse" was one of the many nicknames hung on Cliff because of his large ears.

## RIZZUTO, PHIL (1917-2007)

Phil spent 40 years as a Yankees announcer. He once fled the broadcast booth, leaving an open microphone, to escape a bee.

## ROBINSON, WILBERT "UNCLE ROBBIE" (1863-1934)

On June 10, 1892, Robinson got 7 base hits in a 9-inning game. Not until 1975 did another player (Rennie Stennet of the Pirates) equal his performance.

## SCHRIVER, WILLIAM "POP" (1865-1932)

Although best known as a catcher, Pop played every position on the diamond, except pitcher, during his big-league career.

## SEYBOLD, RALPH "SOCKS" (1870-1921)

Socks hit 16 home runs in 1902. That stood as the American League record until Babe Ruth hit 29 for the 1919 Boston Red Sox.

## SHEPARD, BERT (1920-2008)

Bert never let his artificial leg slow him down. He walked 18 holes of golf several times a week until he was 80.

## SIMON, RANDALL (1975-   )

Talk about returning to the scene of the crime. Simon tried out with the Brewers in 2007. No sausages were harmed.

## SPRINZ, JOSEPH (1902-1994)

Stubborn enough to try and catch a ball dropped from a blimp, Joe's unsurprising nickname was "Mule."

## STENGEL, CHARLES "CASEY" (1890-1975)

Casey was famous for mangling the English language. While managing the Yankees, he once directed his players to, "Line up alphabetically according to height."

## WADDELL, GEORGE "RUBE" (1876-1914)

Rube carried sacks of peanuts in his uniform pockets and threw them to kids in the stands.

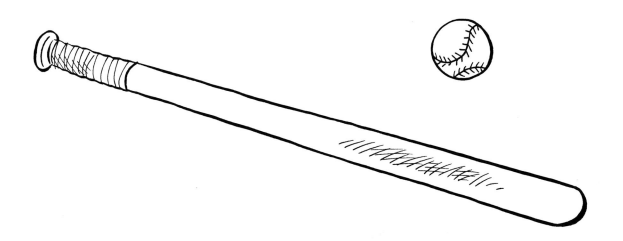